IN SEARCH OF GOD

AND OTHER POEMS

IN SEARCH OF GOD

AND OTHER POEMS

SWAMI VIVEKANANDA

GenNext Publication

Published by

GenNext Publication
5, Ansari Road
New Delhi-110002

Distribution Network
gyanbooks.com
India, USA, Canada, UK, Australia, France

ISBN: 978-93-5663-238-7 (PB)

15 impression 2024

Printed at: Goyal Offset Printers, Delhi.

CONTENTS

SECTION - I

ORIGINAL IN ENGLISH

IN SEARCH OF GOD

O'er hill and dale and mountain range,
In temple, church, and mosque,
In Vedas, Bible, Al Koran
I had searched for Thee in vain.
Like a child in the wildest forest lost
I have cried and cried alone,
'Where art Thou gone, my God, my love?'
The echo answered, 'gone.'

And days and nights and years then passed –
A fire was in the brain;
I knew not when day changed in night,
The heart seemed rent in twain.
I laid me down on Gangâ's shore,
Exposed to sun and rain;
With burning tears I laid the dust
And wailed with waters' roar.

I called on all the holy names
Of every clime and creed,
'Show me the way, in mercy, ye
Great ones who have reached the goal'.

Years then passed in bitter cry,
Each moment seemed an age,
Till one day midst my cries and groans
Some one seemed calling me.

A gentle soft and soothing voice
That said 'my son', 'my son',
That seemed to thrill in unison
With all the chords of my soul.

I stood on my feet and tried to find
The place the voice came from;
I searched and searched and turned to see
Round me, before, behind.
Again, again it seemed to speak –
The voice divine to me.
In rapture all my soul was hushed,
Entranced, enthralled in bliss.

A flash illumined all my soul;
The heart of my heart opened wide.
O joy, O bliss, what do I find!
My love, my love, you are here,
And you are here, my love, my all!

And I was searching thee!
From all eternity you were there
Enthroned in majesty!

From that day forth, where'er I roam,
I feel Him standing by
O'er hill and dale, high mount and vale,
Far far away and high.

The moon's soft light, the stars so bright,
The glorious orb of day,
He shines in them; His beauty – might –
Reflected lights are they.
The majestic morn, the melting eve,
The boundless billowy sea,
In nature's beauty, songs of birds,
I see through them – it is He.

When dire calamity seizes me,
The heart seems weak and faint,
All nature seems to crush me down,
With laws that never bend.

Meseems I hear Thee whispering sweet,
'My love, I am near', 'I am near'.
My heart gets strong. With Thee, my love,

A thousand deaths no fear.
Thou speakest in the mother 's lay
That shuts the baby's eye;
When innocent children laugh and play
I see Thee standing by.

When holy friendship shakes the hand,
He stands between them too;
He pours the nectar in mother's kiss
And the baby's sweet 'mama'.
Thou wert my God with prophets old;
All creeds do come from Thee;
The Vedas, Bible, and Koran bold
Sing Thee in harmony.

'Thou art', 'Thou art' the Soul of souls
In the rushing stream of life.
'Om Tat Sat Om.'[1] Thou art my God.
My love, I am Thine, I am Thine.

THE SONG OF THE FREE

The wounded snake its hood unfurls,
The flame stirred up doth blaze,
The desert air resounds the calls
Of heart-struck lion's rage:

The cloud puts forth its deluge strength
When lightning cleaves its breast,
When the soul is stirred to its inmost depth
Great ones unfold their best!

Let eyes grow dim and heart grow faint,
And friendship fail and love betray,
Let Fate its hundred horrors send
And clotted darkness block the way–

All nature wear one angry frown,
To crush you out – still know, my soul,

1. Tat Sat means that only real existence. [Swamiji's note]

You are Divine. March on and on.
Nor right nor left, but to the goal!

Nor angel I, nor man nor brute,
Nor body, mind, nor he or she;
The books do stop in wonder mute
To tell my nature– I am He!

Before the sun, the moon, the earth,
Before the stars or comets free.
Before e'en time has had its birth–
I was, I am, and I will be!

The beauteous earth, the glorious sun,
The calm sweet moon, the spangled sky,
Causation's laws do make them run;
They live in bonds, in bonds they die–

And mind its mantle, dreamy net,
Cast o'er them all and holds them fast.
In warp and woof of thought are set,
Earth, hells, and heavens, or worst or best.

Know these are but the outer crust –
All space and time, all effect, cause.
I am beyond all sense, all thoughts,
The witness of the universe.

Not two or many, 'tis but one,
And thus in me all me's I have;
I cannot hate, I cannot shun
Myself from me, I can but love.

From dreams awake, from bonds be free,
Be not afraid. This mystery,
My shadow, cannot frighten me,
Know once for all that I am He.

MISUNDERSTOOD

In days of yore
On Ganga's shore preaching,

A hoary priest was teaching–
How Gods they come
As Sitâ Râm,
And gentle Sita pining, weeping.

The sermons end,
They homeward wend their way –
The hearers musing, thinking.

When from the crowd
A voice aloud
This question asked beseeching, seeking –
'Sir, tell me, pray,
Who were but they
These Sita Ram you were teaching, speaking!'

So Mary Hale,
Allow me tell–
You mar my doctrines wronging, baulking.
I never taught
Such queer thought
That all was God – unmeaning talking!

But this I say,
Remember pray,
That God is *true*, all else is *nothing*,
This world's a dream
Though true it seem.
And only truth is *He* the living!
The real *me* is none but *He*
And never, never *matter* changing!

MY PLAY IS DONE

Ever rising, ever falling with the waves of time,
still rolling on I go
From fleeting scene to scene ephemeral,
with life's currents' ebb and flow.
Oh! I am sick of this unending farce;
these shows they please no more.

This ever running, never reaching,
nor e'en a distant glimpse of shore!
From life to life I'm waiting at the gates,
alas, they open not.
Dim are my eyes with vain attempt
to catch one ray long sought.
On little life's high, narrow bridge
I stand and see below
The struggling, crying, laughing throng.
For what? No one can know.
In front yon gates stand frowning dark,
and say: 'No farther way,
This is the limit; tempt not Fate,
bear it as best you may;
Go, mix with them and drink this cup
and be as mad as they.
Who dares to know but comes to grief;
stop then, and with them stay.'
Alas for me. I cannot rest.
This floating bubble, earth –
Its hollow form, its hollow name,
its hollow death and birth –
For me is nothing. How I long
to get beyond the crust
Of name and form! Ah! ope the gates;
to me they open must.
Open the gates of light, O Mother, to me Thy tired son.
I long, oh, long to return home!
Mother, my play is done.
You sent me out in the dark to play,
and wore a frightful mask;
Then hope departed, terror came,
and play became a task.
Tossed to and fro, from wave to wave
in this seething, surging sea
Of passions strong and sorrows deep,
grief is, and joy to be,
Where life is living death, alas! and death –
who knows but 'tis

Another start, another round of this old wheel
of grief and bliss?
Where children dream bright, golden dreams,
too soon to find them dust,
And aye look back to hope long lost
and life a mass of rust!
Too late, the knowledge age cloth gain;
scarce from the wheel we're gone
When fresh, young lives put their strength
to the wheel, which thus goes on
From day to day and year to year.
'Tis but delusion's toy,
False hope its motor; desire, nave;
its spokes are grief and joy.
I go adrift and know not whither.
Save me from this fire!
Rescue me, merciful Mother, from floating with desire!
Turn not to me Thy awful face,
'tis more than I can bear.
Be merciful and kind to me,
to chide my faults forbear.
Take me, O Mother, to those shores
where strifes for ever cease;
Beyond all sorrows, beyond tears,
beyond e'en earthly bliss;
Whose glory neither sun, nor moon,
nor stars that twinkle bright,
Nor flash of lightning can express.
They but reflect its light.
Let never more delusive dreams
veil off Thy face from me.
My play is done, O Mother,
break my chains and make me free!

NO ONE TO BLAME

The sun goes down, its crimson rays
Light up the dying day;

A startled glance I throw behind
And count my triumph shame;
No one but me to blame.

Each day my life I make or mar,
Each deed begets its kind,
Good good, bad bad, the tide once set
No one can stop or stem;
No one but me to blame.

I am my own embodied past;
Therein the plan was made;
The will, the thought, to that conform,
To that the outer frame;
No one but me to blame.

Love comes reflected back as love,
Hate breeds more fierce hate,
They mete their measures, lay on me
Through life and death their claim;
No one but me to blame.

I cast off fear and vain remorse,
I feel my Karma's sway
I face the ghosts my deeds have raised –
Joy, sorrow, censure, fame;
No one but me to blame.

Good, bad, love, hate, and pleasure, pain–
Forever linked go,
I dream of pleasure without pain,
It never, never came;
No one but me to blame.

I give up hate, I give up love,
My thirst for life is gone;
Eternal death is what I want,
Nirvanam goes life's flame;
No one is left to blame.

One only man, one only God, one ever perfect soul,
One only sage who ever scorned the dark and dubious ways,
One only man who dared think and dared show the goal –
That death is curse, and so is life, and best when stops to be.

Om Nama Bhagavate Sambuddhâya
Om, I salute the Lord, the awakened.

THE CUP

This is your cup – the cup assigned to you from the beginning.
Nay, My child, I know how much of that dark drink is your own brew
Of fault and passion, ages long ago,
In the deep years of yesterday, I know.

This is your road – a painful road and drear.
I made the stones that never give you rest.
I set your friend in pleasant ways and clear,
And he shall come like you, unto My breast.

But you, My child, must travel here.
This is your task. It has no joy nor grace,
But it is not meant for any other hand,
And in My universe bath measured place,
Take it. I do not bid you understand.
I bid you close your eyes to see My face.

HOLD ON YET A WHILE, BRAVE HEART

If the sun by the cloud is hidden a bit,
If the welkin shows but gloom,
Still hold on yet a while, brave heart,
The victory is sure to come.

No winter was but summer came behind,
Each hollow crests the wave,

They push each other in light and shade;
Be steady then and brave.

The duties of life are sore indeed,
And its pleasures fleeting, vain,
The goal so shadowy seems and dim,
Yet plod on through the dark, brave heart,
With all thy might and main.

Not a work will be lost, no struggle vain,
Though hopes be blighted, powers gone;
Of thy loins shall come the heirs to all,
Then hold on yet a while, brave soul,
No good is e'er undone.

Though the good and the wise in life are few,
Yet theirs are the reins to lead,
The masses know but late the worth;
Heed none and gently guide.

With thee are those who see afar,
With thee is the Lord of might,
All blessings pour on thee, great soul,
To thee may all come right!

THE SONG OF THE SANNYÂSIN

Wake up the note! the song that had its birth
Far off, where worldly taint could never reach,
In mountain caves and glades of forest deep,
Whose calm no sigh for lust or wealth or fame
Could ever dare to break; where rolled the stream
Of knowledge, truth, and bliss that follows both.
Sing high that note, Sannyâsin bold! Say –
'Om Tat Sat, Om!'

Strike off thy fetters! Bonds that bind thee down,
Of shining gold, or darker, baser ore;
Love, hate – good, bad – and all the dual throng,

Know, slave is slave, caressed or whipped, not free;
For fetters, though of gold, are not less strong to bind;
Then, off with them, Sannyâsin bold! Say –
'Om Tat Sat, Om!'

Let darkness go; the will-o'-the-wisp that leads
With blinking light to pile more gloom on gloom.
This thirst for life, for ever quench; it drags
From birth to death, and death to birth, the soul.
He conquers all who conquers self. Know this
And never yield, Sannyâsin bold! Say –
'Om Tat Sat, Om!'

'Who sows must reap,' they say, 'and cause must bring
The sure effect; good, good; bad, bad; and none
Escape the law. But whoso wears a form
Must wear the chain.' Too true; but far beyond
Both name and form is Âtman, ever free.
Know thou art That, Sannyâsin bold! Say –
'Om Tat Sat, Om!'

They know not truth who dream such vacant dreams
As father, mother, children, wife, and friend.
The sexless Self! whose father He? whose child?
Whose friend, whose foe is He who is but One?
The Self is all in all, none else exists;
And thou art That, Sannyâsin bold! Say –
'Om Tat Sat, Om!'

There is but One – The Free – The Knower – Self!
Without a name, without a form or stain.
In Him is Mâyâ, dreaming all this dream.
The witness, He appears as nature, soul.
Know thou art That, Sannyâsin bold! Say –
'Om Tat Sat, Om!'

Where seekest thou? That freedom, friend, this world
Nor that can give. In books and temples vain
Thy search. Thine only is the hand that holds

The rope that drags thee on. Then cease lament,
Let go thy hold, Sannyâsin bold! Say –
'Om Tat Sat, Om!'

Say, 'Peace to all: From me no danger be
To aught that lives. In those that dwell on high,
In those that lowly creep, I am the Self in all!
All life both here and there, do I renounce,
All heavens and earths and hells, all hopes and fears.'
Thus cut thy bonds, Sannyâsin bold! Say –
'Om Tat Sat, Om!'

Heed then no more how body lives or goes,
Its task is done. Let Karma float it down;
Let one put garlands on, another kick
This frame; say naught. No praise or blame can be
Where praiser praised, and blamer blamed are–one.
Thus be thou calm, Sannyâsin bold! Say –
'Om Tat Sat, Om!'

Truth never comes where lust and fame and greed
Of gain reside. No man who thinks of woman
As his wife can ever perfect be;
Nor he who owns the least of things, nor he
Whom anger chains, can ever pass thro' Maya's gates.
So, give these up, Sannyâsin bold! Say –
'Om Tat Sat, Om!'

Have thou no home. What home can hold thee, friend?
The sky thy roof, the grass thy bed; and food
What chance may bring, well cooked or ill, judge not.
No food or drink can taint that noble Self
Which knows Itself. Like rolling river free
Thou ever be, Sannyâsin bold! Say –
'Om Tat Sat, Om!'

Few only know the truth. The rest will hate
And laugh at thee, great one; but pay no heed.
Go thou, the free, from place to place, and help

Them out of darkness, Maya's veil. Without
The fear of pain or search for pleasure, go
Beyond them both, Sannyâsin bold! Say –
'Om Tat Sat, Om!'

Thus, day by day, till Karma's powers spent
Release the soul for ever. No more is birth,
Nor I, nor thou, nor God, nor man. The 'I'
Has All become, the All is 'I' and Bliss.
Know thou art That, Sannyâsin bold! Say –
'Om Tat Sat, Om!'

TO AN EARLY VIOLET

What though thy bed be frozen earth,
Thy cloak the chilling blast;
What though no mate to cheer thy path,
Thy sky with gloom o'ercast;

What though if love itself doth fail,
Thy fragrance strewed in vain;
What though if bad o'er good prevail,
And vice o'er virtue reign:

Change not thy nature, gentle bloom,
Thou violet, sweet and pure,
But ever pour thy sweet perfume
Unasked, unstinted, sure!

THE LIVING GOD

He who is in you and outside you,
Who works through all hands,
Who walks on all feet,
Whose body are all ye,
Him worship, and break all other idols!

He who is at once the high and low,
The sinner and the saint,
Both God and worm,

Him worship – visible, knowable, real, omnipresent,
Break all other idols!

In whom is neither past life
Nor future birth nor death,
In whom we always have been
And always shall be one,
Him worship. Break all other idols!

Ye fools! who neglect the living God,
And His infinite reflections with which the world is full.
While ye run after imaginary shadows,
That lead alone to fights and quarrels,
Him worship, the only visible!
Break all other idols!

REQUIESCAT IN PACE

Speed forth, O Soul! upon thy star-strewn path;
Speed, blissful one! where thought is ever free,
Where time and space no longer mist the view,
Eternal peace and blessings be with thee!

Thy service true, complete thy sacrifice,
Thy home the heart of love transcendent find;
Remembrance sweet, that kills all space and time,
Like altar roses fill thy place behind!

Thy bonds are broke, thy quest in bliss is found,
And one with That which comes as Death and Life;
Thou helpful one! unselfish e'er on earth,
Ahead! still help with love this world of strife!

TO THE AWAKENED INDIA

Once more awake!
For sleep it was, not death, to bring thee life
Anew, and rest to lotus-eyes for visions
Daring yet. The world in need awaits, O Truth!
No death for thee!

Resume thy march,
With gentle feet that would not break the
Peaceful rest, even of the roadside dust
That lies so low. Yet strong and steady,
Blissful, bold, and free. Awakener, ever
Forward! Speak thy stirring words.

Thy home is gone,
Where loving hearts had brought thee up and
Watched with joy thy growth. But Fate is strong –
This is the law – all things come back to the source
They sprung, their strength to renew.

Then start afresh
From the land of thy birth, where vast cloud-belted
Snows do bless and put their strength in thee,
For working wonders new. The heavenly
River tune thy voice to her own immortal song;
Deodar shades give thee eternal peace.

And all above,
Himala's daughter Umâ, gentle, pure,
The Mother that resides in all as Power
And Life, who works all works and
Makes of One the world, whose mercy
Opens the gate to Truth and shows
The One in All, give thee untiring
Strength, which is Infinite Love.

They bless thee all,
The seers great, whom age nor clime
Can claim their own, the fathers of the
Race, who felt the heart of Truth the same,
And bravely taught to man ill-voiced or
Well. Their servant, thou hast got
The secret – 'tis but One.

Then speak, O Love!
Before thy gentle voice serene, behold how
Visions melt and fold on fold of dreams

Departs to void, till Truth and Truth alone
In all its glory shines –

And tell the world –
Awake, arise, and dream no more!
This is the land of dreams, where Karma
Weaves unthreaded garlands with our thoughts
Of flowers sweet or noxious, and none
Has root or stem, being born in naught, which
The softest breath of Truth drives back to
Primal nothingness. Be bold, and face
The Truth! Be one with it! Let visions cease,
Or, if you cannot, dream but truer dreams,
Which are Eternal Love and Service Free.

TO THE FOURTH OF JULY

Behold, the dark clouds melt away,
That gathered thick at night, and hung
So like a gloomy pall above the earth!
Before thy magic touch, the world
Awakes. The birds in chorus sing.
The flowers raise their star-like crowns –
Dew-set, and wave thee welcome fair.
The lakes are opening wide in love
Their hundred thousand lotus-eyes
To welcome thee, with all their depth.
All hail to thee, thou Lord of Light!
A welcome new to thee, today,
O Sun! Today thou sheddest Liberty!

Bethink thee how the world did wait,
And search for thee, through time and clime.
Some gave up home and love of friends,
And went in quest of thee, self-banished,
Through dreary oceans, through primeval forests,
Each step a struggle for their life or death;
Then came the day when work bore fruit,
And worship, love, and sacrifice,

Fulfilled, accepted, and complete.
  Then thou, propitious, rose to shed
  The light of Freedom on mankind.

Move on, O Lord, in thy resistless path!
Till thy high noon o'erspreads the world.
Till every land reflects thy light,
Till men and women, with uplifted head,
  Behold their shackles broken, and
  Know, in springing joy, their life renewed!

KALI THE MOTHER

The stars are blotted out,
  The clouds are covering clouds,
It is darkness vibrant, sonant.
  In the roaring, whirling wind
Are the souls of a million lunatics
  Just loose from the prison-house,
Wrenching trees by the roots,
  Sweeping all from the path.
The sea has joined the fray,
  And swirls up mountain-waves,
To reach the pitchy sky.
  The flash of lurid light
Reveals on every side
  A thousand, thousand shades
Of Death begrimed and black –
  Scattering plagues and sorrows,
Dancing mad with joy,
  Come, Mother, come!

For Terror is Thy name,
  Death is in Thy breath,
And every shaking step
  Destroys a world for e'er.
Thou 'Time',[1] the All-Destroyer!
  Come, O Mother, come!

1. Kali

Who dares misery love,
And hug the form of Death,
Dance in Destruction's dance,
To him the Mother comes.

ANGELS UNAWARES

I

One bending low with load of life –
That meant no joy, but suffering harsh and hard –
And wending on his way through dark and dismal paths
Without a flash of light from brain or heart
To give a moment's cheer, till the line
That marks out pain from pleasure, death from life,
And good from what is evil was well-nigh wiped from sight,
Saw, one blessed night, a faint but beautiful ray of light
Descend to him. He knew not what or wherefrom,
But called it God and worshipped.

Hope, an utter stranger, came to him and spread
Through all his parts, and life to him meant more
Than he could ever dream and covered all he knew,
Nay, peeped beyond his world. The Sages
Winked, and smiled, and called it 'superstition'.
But he did feel its power and peace
And gently answered back –
'O Blessed Superstition! '

II

One drunk with wine of wealth and power
And health to enjoy them both, whirled on
His maddening course, till the earth, he thought,
Was made for him, his pleasure-garden, and man,
The crawling worm, was made to find him sport,
Till the thousand lights of joy, with pleasure fed,
That flickered day and night before his eyes,
With constant change of colours, began to blur
His sight, and cloy his senses; till selfishness,

Like a horny growth, had spread all o'er his heart;
And pleasure meant to him no more than pain,
Bereft of feeling; and life in the sense,
So joyful, precious once, a rotting corpse between his arms,
Which he forsooth would shun, but more he tried, the more
It clung to him; and wished, with frenzied brain,
A thousand forms of death, but quailed before the charm.

Then sorrow came – and Wealth and Power went –
And made him kinship find with all the human race
In groans and tears, and though his friends would laugh,
His lips would speak in grateful accents –
'O Blessed Misery!'

III

One born with healthy frame – but not of will
That can resist emotions deep and strong,
Nor impulse throw, surcharged with potent strength –
And just the sort that pass as good and kind,
Beheld that he was safe, whilst others long
And vain did struggle 'gainst the surging waves.

Till, morbid grown, his mind could see, like flies
That seek the putrid part, but what was bad.
Then Fortune smiled on him, and his foot slipped.
That ope'd his eyes for e'er, and made him find
That stones and trees ne'er break the law,
But stones and trees remain; that man alone
Is blest with power to fight and conquer Fate,
Transcending bounds and laws.

From him his passive nature fell, and life appeared
As broad and new, and broader, newer grew,
Till light ahead began to break, and glimpse of That
Where Peace Eternal dwells – yet one can only reach
By wading through the sea of struggles – courage-giving, came.

Then looking back on all that made him kin
To stocks and stones, and on to what the world

Had shunned him for, his fall, he blessed the fall,
And with a joyful heart, declared it –
'Blessed Sin!'

TO MY OWN SOUL

Hold yet a while, Strong Heart,
Not part a lifelong yoke
Though blighted looks the present, future gloom.

And age it seems since you and I began our
March up hill or down. Sailing smooth o'er
Seas that are so rare –
Thou nearer unto me, than oft-times I myself –
Proclaiming mental moves before they were!

Reflector true – Thy pulse so timed to mine,
Thou perfect note of thoughts, however fine –
Shall we now part, Recorder, say?
In thee is friendship, faith,
For thou didst warn when evil thoughts were brewing –
And though, alas, thy warning thrown away,
Went on the same as ever – good and true.

PEACE

Behold, it comes in might,
The power that is not power,
The light that is in darkness,
The shade in dazzling light.

It is joy that never spoke,
And grief unfelt, profound,
Immortal life unlived,
Eternal death unmourned.

It is not joy nor sorrow,
But that which is between,
It is not night nor morrow,
But that which joins them in.

It is sweet rest in music;
    And pause in sacred art;
The silence between speaking;
    Between two fits of passion –
    It is the calm of heart.

It is beauty never seen,
    And love that stands alone,
It is song that lives un-sung,
    And knowledge never known.

It is death between two lives,
    And lull between two storms,
The void whence rose creation,
    And that where it returns.

To it the tear-drop goes,
    To spread the smiling form
It is the Goal of Life,
    And Peace – its only home!

WHO KNOWS HOW MOTHER PLAYS!

Perchance a prophet thou –
    Who knows? Who dares touch
The depths where Mother hides
    Her silent failless bolts!

Perchance the child had glimpse
    Of shades, behind the scenes,
With eager eyes and strained,
    Quivering forms – ready
To jump in front and be
    Events, resistless, strong.
Who knows but Mother, how,
    And where, and when, they come?

Perchance the shining sage
    Saw more than he could tell;

Who knows, what soul, and when,
    The Mother makes Her throne?
What law would freedom bind?
    What merit guide Her will,
Whose freak is greatest order,
    Whose will resistless law?
To child may glories ope
    Which father never dreamt;
May thousandfold in daughter
    Her powers Mother store.

THOU BLESSED DREAM

If things go ill or well –
If joy rebounding spreads the face,
Or sea of sorrow swells –
It is a dream, a play.
A play – we each have part,
Each one to weep or laugh as may;
Each one his dress to don –
Alternate shine or rain.

Thou dream, O blessed dream!
Spread far and near thy veil of haze,
Tone down the lines so sharp,
Make smooth what roughness seems.

No magic but in thee!
Thy touch makes desert bloom to life.
Harsh thunder, sweetest song,
Fell death, the sweet release.

A BENEDICTION

The mother's heart, the hero's will,
    The sweetness of the southern breeze,
The sacred charm and strength that dwell
    On Aryan altars, flaming, free;

All these be yours, and many more
No ancient soul could dream before –
Be thou to India's future son
The mistress, servant, friend in one.

MANY HAPPY RETURNS

The mother's heart, the hero's will,
The softest flower's sweetest feel;
The charm and force that ever sway
The altar fire's flaming play;
The strength that leads, in love obeys;
Far-reaching dreams, and patient ways,
Eternal faith in Self, in all
The sight Divine in great in small;
All these, and more than I could see
Today may 'Mother' grant to thee.

LIGHT

I look behind and after
And find that all is right,
In my deepest sorrows
There is a soul of light.

SECTION - II

TRANSLATED FROM SWAMIJI

ON THE SEA'S BOSOM

In blue sky floats a multitude of clouds –
    White, black, of many shades and thicknesses;
An orange sun, about to say farewell,
    Touches the massed cloud-shapes with streaks of red.

The wind blows as it lists, a hurricane
    Now carving shapes, now breaking them apart:
Fancies, colours, forms, inert creations –
    A myriad scenes, though real, yet fantastic.

There light clouds spread, heaping up spun cotton;
    See next a huge snake, then a strong lion;
Again, behold a couple locked in love.
    All vanish, at last, in the vapoury sky.

Below, the sea sings a varied music,
    But not grand, O India, nor ennobling:
Thy waters, widely praised, murmur serene
    In soothing cadence, without a harsh roar.

A SONG OF CREATION

One Mass, devoid of form, name, and colour,
Timeless, devoid of time past and future,
Spaceless, voiceless, boundless, devoid of all –
Where rests hushed even speech of negation.[1]

---

1. 'Neti, Neti,' 'Not this, not this.' Brahman cannot be described in any other positive way.

From thence, down floweth the river causal,
Wearing the form of desire radiant,
Its heaving waters angrily roaring
The constant roar, 'I am', 'I am', 'I am'.

In that ocean of desire limitless,
Appear shining waves, countless, infinite,
Oh, of what power manifold they are,
Of what forms myriad, of what repose,
Of what movements varied, who can reckon?

Millions of moons, millions of suns,
Taking their birth in that very ocean,
Rushing headlong with din tumultuous,
Overspread the whole firmament, drowning
The points of heaven in light effulgent.

In it arise and reside what beings,
Quick with life, dull, and lifeless – unnumbered,
And pleasure and pain, disease, birth, and death!
Verily, the Sun is He, His the ray,
Nay, the Sun is He, and He is the ray.

A SONG ON SAMADHI

Lo! The sun is not, nor the comely moon,
All light extinct; in the great void of space
Floats shadow-like the image-universe.

In the void of mind involute, there floats
The fleeting universe, rises and floats,
Sinks again, ceaseless, in the current 'I'.

Slowly, slowly, the shadow-multitude
Entered the primal womb, and flowed ceaseless,
The only current, the 'I am', 'I am'.

Lo! 'Tis stopped, ev'n that current flows no more,
Void merged into void – beyond speech and mind!
Whose heart understands, he verily does.

SHIVA IN ECSTASY

There Shiva dances, striking both His cheeks; and they resound, *Ba-ba-bom!*
Dimi-dimi-dimi! sounds His tabor; a garland of skulls from His neck is hanging!
In His matted locks the Ganga roars; fire shoots from His mighty trident!
Round His waist a serpent glitters, and on his brow the moon is shining!

THE DANCE OF SHIVA

Lo, the Great God is dancing
–Shiva the all-destroyer and Lord of Creation,
The Master of Yoga and the wielder of Pinaka.[1]

His flaming locks have filled the sky,
Seven worlds play the rhythm
As the trembling earth sways almost to dissolution,
Lo, the Great God Shiva is dancing.

TO SHRI KRISHNA

O Krishna, my friend, let me go to the water,
O let me go today.
Why play tricks with one who is already thy slave?
O friend, let me go today, let me go.
I have to fill my pitcher in the waters of the Yamuna.
I pray with folded hands, friend, let me go.

TO A FRIEND

Where darkness is interpreted as light,
Where misery passes for happiness,
Where disease is pretended to be health,
Where the new-born's cry but shows 'tis alive;
Dost thou, O wise, expect happiness here?

1. Trident.

Where war and competition ceaseless run,
Even the father turns against the son,
Where 'self', 'self' – this always the only note,
Dost thou, O wise, seek for peace supreme here?

A glaring mixture of heaven and hell,
Who can fly from this Samsâr[1] of Mâyâ?
Fastened in the neck with Karma's fetters,
Say, where can the slave escape for safety?

The paths of Yoga and of sense-enjoyment,
The life of the householder and Sannyâs,
Devotion, worship, and earning riches,
Vows, Tyâga, and austerities severe,
I have seen through them all. What have I known?

– Have known there's not a jot of happiness,
Life is only a cup of Tantalus;[2]
The nobler is your heart, know for certain,
The more must be your share of misery.

Thou large-hearted Lover unselfish, know,
There's no room in this sordid world for thee;
Can a marble figure e'er brook the blow
That an iron mass can afford to bear?

Couldst thou be as one inert and abject,
Honey-mouthed, but with poison in thy heart,
Destitute of truth and worshipping self,
Then thou wouldst have a place in this Samsar.

Pledging even life for gaining knowledge,
I have devoted half my days on earth;

1. Samsâra, the world.
2. A scientific toy consisting of a cup with a puppet in its bowl. Water may be poured into the bowl as high as the puppet's chin, and then it will recede, being let out at the bottom through a siphon concealed in the puppet's body. (Tantalus, a wealthy king and son of Zeus, was punished in the lower world by being condemned to stand in water up to the chin and beneath fruit-laden branches, with water and fruit receding at each attempt to drink or eat.)

For the sake of love, even as one insane,
I have often clutched at shadows lifeless;

For religion, many creeds have I sought,
Lived in mountain-caves, on cremation-grounds,
By the Ganga and other sacred streams,
And how many days have I passed on alms!

Friendless, clad in rags, with no possession,
Feeding from door to door on what chance would bring.
The frame broken under Tapasyâ's[1] weight;
What riches, ask thou, have I earned in life?

Listen, friend, I will speak my heart to thee;
I have found in my life this truth supreme –
Buffeted by waves, in this whirl of life,
There's one ferry that takes across the sea[2]

Formulas of worship, control of breath,
Science, philosophy, systems varied,
Relinquishment, possession, and the like,
All these are but delusions of the mind –
Love, Love – that's the one thing, the sole treasure.

In Jiva and Brahman, in man and God,
In ghosts, and wraiths, and spirits, and so forth,
In Devas, beasts, birds, insects, and in worms,
This Prema[3] dwells in the heart of them all.

Say, who else is the highest God of gods?
Say, who else moves all the universe?
The mother dies for her young, robber robs –
Both are but the impulse of the same Love!

Beyond the ken of human speech and mind,
It dwells in weal and woe; 'tis that which comes

1. Austerities.
2. The sea of Samsara.
3. Love.

As the all-powerful, all-destroyer
Kâli, and as the kindliest mother.

Disease, bereavement, pinch of poverty,
Dharma,[1] and its opposite Adharma,[2]
Are but ITS worship in manifold modes;
Say, what does by himself a Jiva do?

Deluded is he who happiness seeks,
Lunatic he who misery wishes,
Insane he too who fondly longs for death,
Immortality – vain aspiration!

Far, far, however far you may travel,
Mounted on the brilliant mental car,
'Tis the same ocean of the Samsar,
Happiness and misery whirling on.

Listen O Vihangam,[3] bereft of wings,
'Tis not the way to make good your escape;
Time and again you get blows, and collapse,
Why then attempt what is impossible?

Let go your vain reliance on knowledge,
Let go your prayers, offerings, and strength,
For Love selfless is the only resource;–
Lo, the insects teach, embracing the flame!

The base insect's blind, by beauty charmed,
Thy soul is drunken with the wine of Love;
O thou Lover true, cast into the fire
All thy dross of self, thy mean selfishness.

Say – comes happiness e'er to a beggar?
What good being object of charity?
Give away, ne'er turn to ask in return,
Should there be the wealth treasured in thy heart.

1. Virtue.
2. Vice
3. Bird, here addressed to the bound soul.

Ay, born heir to the Infinite thou art,
Within the heart is the ocean of Love,
'Give', 'Give away' – whoever asks return,
His ocean dwindles down to a mere drop.

From highest Brahman to the yonder worm,
And to the very minutest atom,
Everywhere is the same God, the All-Love;
Friend, offer mind, soul, body, at their feet.

These are His manifold forms before thee,
Rejecting them, where seekest thou for God?
Who loves all beings without distinction,
He indeed is worshipping best his God.

AND LET SHYAMA DANCE THERE

Beaut'ous blossoms ravishing with perfume,
Swarms of maddened bees buzzing all around;
The silver moon – a shower of sweet smile,
Which all the dwellers of heaven above
Shed lavishly upon the homes of earth;

The soft Malaya[1] breeze, whose magic touch
Opens to view distant memory's folds;
Murmuring rivers and brooks, rippling lakes
With restless Bhramaras[2] wheeling over
Gently waving lotuses unnumbered;

Foaming flow cascades – a streaming music –
To which echo mountain caves in return;
Warblers, full of sweet-flowing melody,
Hidden in leaves, pour hearts out – love discourse;

The rising orb of day, the painter divine,
With his golden brush but lightly touches
The canvas earth and a wealth of colours

1. Malaya–a fabulous Sandal-wood mountain in the South. Hence, Malaya breeze means a fragrant breeze from the South.
2. A bettle somewhat like a humble bee, which lives solely on honey.

Floods at once o'er the bosom of nature,
– Truly a museum of lovely hues –
Waking up a whole sea of sentiments.

The roll of thunder, the crashing of clouds,
War of elements spreading earth and sky;
Darkness vomiting forth blinding darkness,
The Pralaya[1] wind angrily roaring;

In quick bursts of dazzling splendour flashes
Blood-red terrific lightning, dealing death;
Monster waves roaring like thunder, foaming,
Rush impetuous to leap mountain peaks;

The earth booms furious, reels and totters,
Sinks down to its ruin, hurled from its place;
Piercing the ground, stream forth tremendous flames.
Mighty ranges blow up into atoms.

A lovely villa, on a lake of blue –
Festooned with dusters of water-lilies;
The heart-blood of ripe grapes capped with white foam
Whispering softly tells tale of passion;

The melody of the harp floods the ears,
And by its air, time, and harmony rich,
Enhances desire in the breast of man;
What stirring of emotions! How many
Hot sighs of Love! And warm tears coursing down!

The Bimba[2]-red lips of the youthful fair,
The two blue eyes – two oceans of feelings;
The two hands eager to advance – love's cage –
In which the heart, like a bird, lies captive.

The martial music bursts, the trumpets blow,
The ground shakes under the warriors' tread;

1. The time of cosmic destruction.
2. A kind of fruit of a rich red colour.

The roar of cannon, the rattle of guns,
Volumes of smoke, the gruesome battlefield–

The thundering artillery vomits fire
In thousand directions; shells burst and strike
Vital parts of the body; elephants
And horses mounted are blown up in space;

The earth trembles under this infernal dance;
A million heroes mounted on steeds
Charge and capture the enemy's ordnance,
Piercing through the smoke and shower of shells–

And rain of bullets; forward goes the flag,
The emblem of victory, of heroism
With the blood, yet hot, streaming down the staff,
Followed by the rifles, drunk with war-spirit;

Lo! the ensign falls, but the flag proceeds
Onwards on the shoulder of another;
Under his feet swell heaps of warriors
Perished in battle; but he falters not.

The flesh hankers for contacts of pleasure,
The senses for enchanting strains of song,
The mind hungers for peals of laughter sweet,
The heart pants to reach realms beyond sorrow;

Say, who cares exchange the soothing moonlight
For the burning rays of the noontide sun?
The wretch whose heart is like the scorching sun,
– Even he fondly loves the balmy moon;

Indeed, all thirst for joy. Breathes there the wretch
Who hugs pain and sorrow to his bosom?
Misery in his cup of happiness,
Deadly venom in his drink of nectar,
Poison in his throat – yet he clings to hope!

Lo! how all are scared by the Terrific,
None seek Elokeshi[1] whose form is Death.
The deadly frightful sword, reeking with blood,
They take from Her hand, and put a lute instead!

Thou dreaded Kâli, the All-destroyer,
Thou alone art true; Thy shadow's shadow
Is indeed the pleasant Vanamâli.[1]
O Terrible Mother, cut quick the core,
Illusion dispel – the dream of happiness,
Rend asunder the fondness for the flesh.

True, they garland Thee with skulls, but shrink back
In fright and call Thee, 'O All-merciful!'
At Thy thunder peal of awful laughter,
At Thy nudeness – for space is thy garment –
Their hearts sink down with terror, but they say,
'It is the demons that the Mother kills!'

They only pretend they wish to see Thee,
But when the time comes, at Thy sight they flee.
Thou art Death! To each and all in the world
Thou distributest the plague and disease
– Vessels of venom filled by Thine own hands.

O thou insane! Thou but cheatest thyself,
Thou dost not turn thy head lest thou behold.
Ay, the form terrible of the Mother.
Thou courtest hardship hoping happiness,
Thou wearest cloak of Bhakti and worship,
With mind full of achieving selfish ends.

The blood from the severed head of a kid
Fills thee with fear – thy heart throbs at the sight –
Verily a coward! Compassionate?[3]

---

1. Literally, He who is garlanded with wild flowers. The Shepherd Krishna in His aspect of youthful sport.
2. The idea is that the brave alone can be compassionate, and not the coward.
3. The wheel of constant birth and death, hence the world.

Bless my soul! A strange state of things indeed!
To whom shall I tell the truth? – Who will see?

Free thyself from the mighty attraction –
The maddening wine of love, the charm of sex.
Break the harp! Forward, with the ocean's cry!
Drink tears, pledge even life – let the body fall.

Awake, O hero! Shake off thy vain dreams,
Death stands at thy head – does fear become thee?
A load of misery, true though it is –
This Becoming[1] – know this to be thy God!
His temple – the Shmashâna among corpses
And funeral pyres; unending battle –
That verily is His sacred worship;
Constant defeat – let that not unnerve thee;
Shattered be little self, hope, name, and fame;
Set up a pyre of them and make thy heart
A burning-ground.
And let Shyâmâ[2] dance there.

A SONG I SING TO THEE

A song I sing. A song I sing to Thee!
Nor care I for men's comments, good or bad.
Censure or praise I hold of no account.
Servant am I, true servant of Thee Both,[3]
Low at Thy feet, with Shakti, I salute!

Thou standest steadfast, ever at my back,
Hence when I turn me round, I see Thy face,
Thy smiling face. Therefore I sing again
And yet again. Therefore I fear no fear;
For birth and death lie prostrate at my feet.

Thy servant am I through birth after birth,
Sea of mercy, inscrutable Thy ways;

1. The cremation ground.
2. The Dark One, Kali.
3. Purusha and Prakriti: Male and female principles.

So is my destiny inscrutable;
It is unknown; nor would I wish to know.
Bhakti, Mukti, Japa, Tapas, all these,
Enjoyment, worship, and devotion too –
These things and all things similar to these,
I have expelled at Thy supreme command.
But only one desire is left in me –
An intimacy with Thee, mutual!
    Take me, O Lord across to Thee;
    Let no desire's dividing line prevent.

The eye looks out upon the universe,
Nor does it seek to look upon itself;
Why should it? It sees itself in others.
    Thou art my eyes! Thou and Thou alone;
    For every living temple shrines Thy face.

Like to the playing of a little child
Is every attitude of mine toward Thee.
Even, at times, I dare be angered with Thee;
Even, at times, I'd wander far away: –
Yet there, in greyest gloom of darkest night,
Yet there, with speechless mouth and tearful eyes,
Thou standest fronting me, and Thy sweet Face
Stoops down with loving look on face of mine.
Then, instantly, I turn me back to Thee,
And at Thy feet I fall on bended knees.
    I crave no pardon at Thy gentle hands,
    For Thou art never angry with Thy son.
Who else with all my foolish freaks would bear?

Thou art my Master! Thou my soul's real mate.
Many a time I see Thee – I am Thee!
Ay, I am Thee, and Thou, my Lord, art me!
Thou art within my speech. Within my throat
Art Thou, as Vinâpâni,[1] learned, wise.
On the flow of Thy current and its force

1. Goddess of learning.

Humanity is carried as Thou wilt.
The thunder of Thy Voice is borne upon the boom
Of crashing waves, of over-leaping seas;
The sun and moon give utterance to Thy Voice;
Thy conversation, in the gentle breeze
Makes itself heard in truth, in very truth,
True! True! And yet, the while, these gross precepts
Give not the message of the Higher Truth
Known to the knower!
                    Lo! The sun, the moon,
The moving planets and the shining stars,
Spheres of abode by myriads in the skies,
The comet swift, the glimmering lightning-flash,
The firmament, expanded, infinite –
These all, observant watchful eyes behold,

Anger, desire, greed, Moha,[1] and the rest,[2]
Whence issues forth the waving of the play
Of this existence; the home wherein dwells
Knowledge, and non-knowledge – whose centre is
The feeling of small self, the 'Aham!' 'Aham!'
Full of the dual sense of pleasure and of pain,
Teeming with birth and life, decay and death,
Whose arms are 'The External' and 'The Internal',
All things that are, down to the ocean's depths,
Up to sun, moon, and stars in spanless space –
The Mind, the Buddhi, Chitta, Ahamkâr,
The Deva, Yaksha, man and demon, all,
The quadruped, the bird, the worm, all insect life,
The atom and its compound, all that is,
Animate and inanimate, all, all –
The Internal and the External – dwell
In that one common plane of existence!
    This outward presentation is of order gross,
    As hair on human brow, Ay! very gross.

1. Delusion.
2. Such as pride and malice, the six passions.

On the spurs of the massive Mount Meru[1]
The everlasting snowy ranges lie,
Extending miles and miles beyond more miles.
Piercing through clouds into the sky above
Its peaks thrust up in hundreds, glorious,
Brilliantly glistening, countless, snowy-white:
Flash upon flash of vivid lightning fleet,
    The sun, high in his northern solstice hung,
With force of thousand rays concentrating,
Pours down upon the mountain floods of heat,
Furious as a billion thunderbolts,
From peak to peak.
    Behold! The radiant sun
Swoons, as it were, in each. Then melts
The massive mountain with its crested peaks!
Down, down, it falls, with a horrific crash!
    Water with water lies commingled now,
    And all has passed like to a passing dream.

When all the many movements of the mind
Are, by Thy grace, made one, and unified,
The light of that unfoldment is so great
That, in its splendour, it surpasses far
The brilliance of ten thousand rising suns.
Then, sooth, the sun of Chit[2] reveals itself.
And melt away the sun and moon and stars,
High heaven above, the nether worlds, and all!
This universe seems but a tiny pool
Held in a hollow caused by some cow's hoof.
    –This is the reaching of the region which
    Beyond the plane of the External lies.

Calmed are the clamours of the urgent flesh,
The tumult of the boastful mind is hushed,
Cords of the heart are loosened and set free,
Unfastened are the bandages that bind,

1. A fabulous mountain round which the planets are said to revolve.
2. Knowledge.

Attachment and delusion are no more!
Ay! There sounds sonorous the Sound
Void of vibration. Verily! Thy Voice!
Hearing that Voice, Thy servant, reverently,
Stands ever ready to fulfil Thy work.

'I exist.
When, at Pralaya time
This wondrous universe is swallowed up;
Knowledge, the knower and the known, dissolved;
The world no more distinguishable, now,
No more conceivable; when sun and moon
And all the outspent stars, remain no more –
Then is the state of Mahâ-Nirvâna,
When action, act, and actor, are no more,
When instrumentality is no more;
Great darkness veils the bosom of the dark –
There I am present.

'I am present!
At Pralaya time,
When this vast universe is swallowed up,
Knowledge, and knower, and the known
Merged into one.
The universe no more
Can be distinguished or can be conceived
By intellect. The sun and moon and stars are not.
Over the bosom of the darkness, darkness moves
Intense Devoid of all the threefold bonds,
Remains the universe. Gunas are calmed
Of all distinctions. Everything deluged
In one homogeneous mass, subtle,
Pure, of atom-form, indivisible –
There I am present.

'Once again,
I unfold Myself – that 'I';
Of My 'Shakti' the first great change is Om;
The Primal Voice rings through the void;

Infinite Space hears that great vibrant sound.
The group of Primal Causes shakes off sleep,
New life revives atoms interminable;
Cosmic existence heaves and whirls and sways,
Dances and gyrates, moves towards the core,
From distances immeasurably far.

The animate Wind arouses rings of Waves
Over the Ocean of great Elements;
Stirring, falling, surging, that vast range of Waves
Rushes with lightning fury. Fragments thrown
By force of royal resistance through the path
Of space, rush, endless, in the form of spheres
Celestial, numberless. Planets and stars
Speed swift; and man's abode, the earth revolves.

'At the Beginning,
I, the Omniscient One,
I am! The moving and the un-moving,
All this Creation comes into being
By the unfoldment of My power supreme.
I play with My own Maya, My Power Divine.
The One, I become the many, to behold
My own Form.

'At the Beginning,
I, the Omniscient One,
I am! The moving and the un-moving,
All this Creation comes into being
By the unfoldment of My power supreme.
Perforce of My command, the wild storm blows
On the face of the earth; clouds clash and roar;
The flash of lightning startles and rebounds;
Softly and gently the Malaya breeze
Flows in and out like calm, unruffled breath;
The moon's rays pour their cooling current forth;
The earth's bare body in fair garb is clothed,
Of trees and creepers multitudinous;

And the flower abloom lifts her happy face,
Washed with drops of dew, towards the sun.'

A HYMN TO THE DIVINE MOTHER

अम्बास्तोत्रम्।

का त्वं शुभकरे सुखदुःखहस्ते
आघूर्णितं भवजलं प्रबलोर्मिभङ्गैः।
शान्ति विधातुमिह किं बहुधा विभग्नाम्
मतः प्रयत्नपरमासि सदैव विश्वे।।

O Thou most beautiful! Whose holy hands
Hold pleasure and hold pain! Doer of good!
Who art Thou? The water of existence
By Thee is whirled and tossed in mighty waves.
Is it, O Mother, to restore again
This universe's broken harmony
That Thou, without cessation, art at work?

संपादयत्यविरतं त्वविरामवृत्ता
या वै स्थिता कृतफलं त्वकृतस्य नेत्री।
सा मे भवत्वनिदिनं वरदा भवानी
जानाम्यहं ध्रुवमिदं धृतकर्मपाशा।।

Oh! May the Mother of the universe –
In whose activity no respite rests,
Incessantly distributing the fruits
Of action done, guiding unceasingly
All action yet to come – bestow Her boon
Of blessing on me, Her child, for evermore.
I realise, I know, that it is Thou
Who holdest in Thy hands dread Karma's ropes.

को वा धर्मः किमकृतं क्वः कपाललेखः
किंवादृष्ट फलमिहास्ति हि यां विना भोः

इच्छापाशैर्नियमिता नियमाः स्वतन्त्रैः
यस्या नेत्री भवति सा शरणं ममाद्या।।

Is it inherent nature? Something uncreate?
Or Destiny? Some unforeseen result? –
Who lacking nothing, is accountable,
Whose chain of will, untrammelled, grasps the laws,
May She, the Primal Guide, my shelter be!

सन्तानयन्ति जलधिं जनिमृत्युजालम
सम्भावयन्त्यविकृतं विकृतं विभग्नम्।
यस्या विभूतय इहामितशक्तिपालाः
नाश्रित्य तां वद कुतः शरणं व्रजामः।।

Manifestations of Her glory show
In power of immeasurable might,
Throughout the universe, powers that swell
The sea of birth and death, forces that change
And break up the Unchanged and changed again.
Lo! Where shall we seek refuge, save in Her?

मित्रे रिपौ त्वविषमं तव पद्मनेत्रम्
स्वस्थे दुःस्थे त्ववितथं तव हस्तपातः।
मृत्युच्छाया तव दया त्वमृतञ्च मातः
मा मां मुञ्चन्तु परमे शुभदृष्टयस्ते।।

To friend and foe Thy lotus-eyes are even;
Ever Thine animating touch brings fruit
To fortunate and unfortunate alike;
The shade of death and immortality –
Both these, O mother, are Thy grace Supreme!
Mother Supreme! Oh, may Thy gracious face
Never be turned away from me, Thy child!

क्वाम्बा सर्वा क्व गणनं मम हीनबुद्धेः
धत्तुं दोर्भ्यामिव मतिर्जगदेकधात्रीम्।।

श्रीसञ्चिन्त्यं सुचरणम भयप्रतिष्ठम्
सेवासारैरभिनुतं शरणं प्रपद्ये।।

What Thou art, the Mother! the All. How praise?
My understanding is so little worth.
'Twere like desire to seize with hands of mine
The sole Supporter of the universe!
So, at Thy blessed feet – contemplated
By the Goddess of Fortune Herself – the abode
Of fearlessness, worshipped by service true –
There, at those blessed feet, I take refuge!

या मामाजन्म विनयत्यतिदुःखमार्गैः
आसंसिद्धेः स्वकलितैर्ल्ललितैर्विलासैः।
मा मे बुद्धिं सुविदधे सततं धरण्यम्
साम्बा सर्वा मम गतिः सफलेऽफले वा।।

She who, since birth, has ever led me on
Through paths of trouble to perfection's goal,
Mother-wise, in Her own sweet playful ways,
She, who has always through my life inspired
My understanding, She, my Mother, She,
The All, is my resort, whether my work
O'erdow with full fruition or with none.

A HYMN TO SHIVA

शिवस्तोत्रम्।
ओं नमः शिवाय।
निखिलभुवनजन्मस्थमभङ्गप्ररोहाः
अकलित महिमानः कल्पिता यत्र तस्मिन्।
सुविमलगगनाभे ईशसंस्थेऽप्यनीशे
मम भवतु भवेऽस्मिन् भासुरो भावबन्धः।।

Salutation to Shiva! whose glory
Is immeasurable, who resembles sky
In clearness, to whom are attributed
The phenomena of all creation,
The preservation and dissolution
Of the universe! May the devotion,
The burning devotion of this my life
Attach itself to Him, to Shiva, who,
While being Lord of all, transcends Himself.

निहतनिखिलमोहेऽधीशता यत्र रूढा
प्रकटितपरप्रेम्णा यो महादेवसंज्ञः।
अशिथिलपरिरंभः प्रेमरूपस्य यस्य
प्रणयति हृदि विश्वं व्याजमात्रं विभुत्वम्।।

In whom Lordship is ever established,
Who causes annihilation of delusion,
Whose most surpassing love, made manifest,
Has crowned Him with a name above all names,
The name of "Mahâdeva", the Great God!
Whose warm embrace, of Love personified,
Displays, within man's heart, that all power
Is but a semblance and a passing show,

वहति विपुलवातः पूर्वसंस्काररूपः
प्रमथति बलवृन्दं धूर्णितेवोर्मिमाला।
प्रचलति खलु युग्मं युष्मदस्मत्प्रतीतं
अतिविकलितरूपं नौमि चित्तं शिवस्थम्।।

In which the tempest of the whole past blows,
Past Samskâras,[1] stirring the energies
With violence, like water lashed to waves;
In which the dual consciousness of "I" and "Thou"
Plays on: I salute that mind unstable,
Centred in Shiva, the abode of calm!

1. The accumulated effects of past desires and actions.

जनकजनितभावो वृत्तयः संस्कृताश्च
अगणनबहुरूपा यत्र एको यथार्थः।
शामितविकृतिवाते यत्र नान्तर्बहिश्च
तमहह हरमीडे चेत्तवृत्तेर्निरोधम्।।

Where the ideas of parent and produced,
Purified thoughts and endless varied forms,
Merge in the Real one; where the existence ends
Of such conceptions as "within", "without" –
The wind of modification being stilled –
That Hara I worship, the suppression
Of movements of the mind. Shiva I hail!

गलिततिमिरमालः शुभ्रतेजःप्रकाशः
धवलकमलशोभः ज्ञानपुञ्जाट्टहासः।
यमिजनहृदिगम्यः निष्कलं ध्यायमानः
प्रणतमवतु मं सः मानसो राजहंसः।।

From whom all gloom and darkness have dispersed
That radiant Light, white, beautiful
As bloom of lotus white is beautiful;
Whose laughter loud sheds knowledge luminous;
Who, by undivided meditation,
Is realised in the self-controlled heart:
May that Lordly Swan of the limpid lake
Of my mind, guard me, prostrate before Him!

दुरितदलनदक्षं दक्षजादत्तदोषं
कलितकलिकलङ्कं कम्रकह्लारकान्तं।
परहितकरणाय प्राणविच्छेदसूत्कं
नतनयननियुक्तं नीलकण्ठं नमामः।।

Him, the Master-remover of evil,
Who wipes the dark stain of this Iron Age;
Whom Daksha's Daughter gave Her coveted hand;
Who, like the charming water-lily white,

Is beautiful; who is ready ever
To part with life for others' good, whose gaze
    Is on the humble fixed; whose neck is blue[1]
With the poison[2] swallowed: Him, we salute!

A HYMN TO THE DIVINITY OF SHRI RAMAKRISHNA

We salute Thee! Lord! Adored of the world,
Samsâra's bondage breaker, taintless Thou,
Embodiment of blessed qualities,
Thou transcendest all Gunas: human form
Thus bearest. Thee we salute and adore!

Refuge of mind and speech, Thou art beyond
The reach of either. Radiance art Thou
In all radiance that is. The heart's cave
Is by Thy visitance resplendent made.
Verily Thou art that which dispelleth
The densest darkness of Tamas in man.

One glancing vision at Thine eyes divine
Cleared by the collyrium of Jnâna
Defies delusion. O thou blotter-out
Of all the taints of sin, Intelligence
Pure, unmingled is Thy form. Of the world
    Thou art embellisher. Self-luminous
Art Thou. O Ocean of feeling sublime,
And of Love Divine, O God-maddened One,
Devotees win Thy blessed feet and cross
Safely the swelling sea of Samsara.

O Lord of the world, though Thy Yoga power
Thou shinest as the Incarnation clear
Of this our time. O thou of strict restraint,
Only through Thine unstinted grace we see
The mind in Samâdhi completely merged;

1. Nilkantha, a name of Shiva.
2. The all-destructive evil.

Mercy Incarnate! austere are Thy deeds.
Thou dealest to the evil of Misery
Destruction. Kali's[1] binding cords
Are cut by Thee asunder. Thine own life
Thou gavest freely, O sweet Sacrifice,
O best of men! O Saviour of the world!

Devoid wert Thou of the idea of sex,
Thought of possession charmed Thee not. To Thee
Obnoxious was all pleasure. Give to us,
O greatest among Tyâgis,[2] love intense
Unto Thy sacred feet; give, we implore!

Fearless art Thou, and past all gloom of doubt;
Thy mind is wrapt in its own firm resolve;
Thy lovers, whose devotion mounts above
The realm of reason, who renounce the pride
Of caste and parentage, of name and fame –
Their safe refuge art Thou alone, O Lord!

My one true treasure is Thy blessed feet,
Reaching which the whole universe itself
Seems like a puddle in the hollow made
By hoof of passing cow. O bestower
To Love! O Seer of equality
In all! O verily, in Thee the pain
And evil of this mortal world escapes,
And vanishes, O cherished One, in Thee!

Lo! In variety of melody
Forth-breaking in fine harmony most sweet,
Hymns of Thy devotees, accompanied
By Mridanga[3] playing with music's grace,
Fill the air, in evening worship to Thee.

---

1. Of the Iron Age.
2. Renouncers.
3. A kind of drum.

WHOM TO FEAR?

कुर्मस्तारकचर्वणं त्रिभुवनमुत्पाटयामो बलात्।
किं भो न विजानास्यस्मान् रामकृष्णदासा वयम्।।

We shall crush the stars to atoms, and unhinge the universe. Don't you know who we are? We are the servants of Shri Ramakrishna.

क्षीणाः स्म दीनाः सकरुणा जल्पन्ति मूढा जना
नास्तिक्यन्त्विदन्तु अहह देहात्मवादातुराः।
प्राप्ताः स्म वीरा गतभया अभयं प्रतिष्ठां यदा
आस्तिक्यन्त्विदन्तु चिनुमः रामकृष्णदासा वयम्।।

It is those foolish people who identify themselves with their bodies, that piteously cry, 'We are weak, we are low.' All this is atheism. Now that we have attained the state beyond fear, we shall have no more fear and become heroes. This indeed is theism which we, the servants of Shri Ramakrishna, will choose.

पीत्वा पीत्वा परमममृतं वीतसंसाररागाः
हित्वा हित्वा सकलकलहप्रापिणीं स्वार्थसिद्धिम्।
ध्यात्वा ध्यात्वा गुरुवरपदं सर्वकल्याणरूपम्
नत्वा नत्वा सकलभुवनं पातुमामन्त्रयामः।।

Giving up the attachment for the world and drinking constantly the supreme nectar of immortality, for ever discarding that self-seeking spirit which is the mother of all dissension, and ever meditating on the blessed feet of our Guru which are the embodiment of all well-being, with repeated salutations we invite the whole world to participate in drinking the nectar.

प्राप्तं यद्वै त्वनादिनिधनं वेदोदधिं मथित्वा
दत्तं यस्य प्रकरणे हरिहरब्रह्मादिदेवैर्बलम्।

पूर्ण यत्तु प्राणसारैर्भौमनारायणानां
रामकृष्णस्तनुं धत्ते तत्पूर्णपात्रमिदं भोः।।

That nectar which has been obtained by churning the infinite ocean of the Vedas, into which Brahmâ, Vishnu, Shiva, and the other gods have poured their strength, which is charged with the life-essence of the Avataras – Gods Incarnate on earth – Shri Ramakrishna holds that nectar in his person, in its fullest measure!

HYMN TO SHRI RAMAKRISHNA

I

ॐ ह्रीं ऋतं त्वमचलो गुणजित् गुणेड्यो
नक्तं दिवं सकरुणं तव पादपद्मम्।
मोहङ्कषं बहुकृतं न भजे यतोऽहं
तस्मात्त्वमेव शरणं मम दीनबन्धो।।1।।

1. Om! Hrim! Thou art the True, the Imperturbable One, transcending the three Gunas and yet adored for Thy virtues! Inasmuch as I do not worship day and night, with yearning, Thy compassionate lotus feet which destroy all ignorance, therefore, O Thou friend of the lowly, Thou art my only refuge.

भक्तिर्भगश्च भजनं भवभेदकारि
गच्छन्त्यलं सुविपुलं गमनाय तत्त्वम्।
वक्तोद्धृ तन्तु हृदि मे न च भाति किंचित्
तस्मात्त्वमेव शरणं मम दीनबन्धो।।2।।

2. Spiritual powers, reverence, and worship which put an end to this cycle of birth and death are enough indeed to lead to the greatest Truth. But this while finding utterance through the mouth is not at all being brought home to my heart. Therefore, O Thou friend of the lowly, Thou art my only refuge.

तेजस्तरन्ति तरसा त्वयि तृप्ततृष्णा:
रागे कृते ऋतपथे त्वयि रामकृष्णे।
मर्त्यामृतं तव पदं मरणोर्मिनाशं
तस्मात्त्वमेव शरणं मम दीनबन्धो।।3।।

3. If devotion is directed to Thee, O Ramakrishna, the way of Divine Truth, then with desires all fulfilled in Thee, they forthwith cross over this sea of Rajas: for Thy feet are like nectar to the mortals, quelling the waves of death. Therefore, O Thou friend of the lowly, Thou art my only refuge.

कृत्यं करोति कलुषं कुहकान्तकारि
ष्णान्तं शिवं सुविमलं तव नाम नाथ।
यस्मादहं त्वशरणो जगदेकगम्य
तस्मात्त्वमेव शरणं मम दीनबन्धो।।4।।

4. O Thou dispeller of illusion, Thy name ending in "shna", pure and auspicious, converts sinfulness to purity. Because, O Thou the only goal of all beings, shelter have I none, therefore Thou art, O friend of the lowly, my only refuge.

II

आचण्डालाप्रतिहतरयो यस्य प्रेमप्रवाह:
लोकातीतोऽप्यहह न जहौ लोककल्याणमार्गम्।
त्रैलोक्येऽप्यप्रतिममहिमा जानकीप्राणबन्धो
भक्त्या ज्ञानं वृतवरवपुः सीतया यो हि रामः।।1।।

1. He who was Shri Rama, whose stream of love flowed with resistless might even to the Chandâla (the outcaste); Oh, who ever was engaged in doing good to the world though superhuman by nature, whose renown there is none to equal in the three worlds, Sitâ's beloved, whose body of Knowledge Supreme was embraced by Sita, who is love-personified.

नरदेव देव जय जय नरदेव।
स्तब्धीकृत्य प्रलयकलितं वाहवोत्थं महान्तं
हित्वा रात्रिं प्रकृतिसहजामन्धतामिस्रमिश्राम्।
गीतं शान्तं मधुरमपि यः सिंहनादं जगर्ज
सोऽयं जातः प्रथितपुरुषो रामकृष्णस्त्विदानीम्
नरदेव देव जय जय नरदेव।।।2।।

2. He who quelled the noise, terrible like that at the time of destruction, arising from the battle (of Kurukshetra), who destroyed the terrible yet natural night of ignorance (of Arjuna) and who roared out the Gita sweet and appeasing; That renowned soul is born now as Shri Ramakrishna.

नरदेव देव जय जय नरदेव।
शक्तिसमुद्रसमुत्थतरङ्गं
दर्शितप्रेमविजृम्भितरङ्गम्।
संशयराक्षसनाशमहास्त्रं
यामि गुरुं शरणं भववैद्यम्।।
नरदेव देव जय जय नरदेव।।3।।

3. Hail, O Lord of Men! Victory unto You! I surrender myself to my Guru, the physician for the malady of Samsâra (relative existence) who is, as it were, a wave rising in the ocean of Shakti (Power), who has shown various sports of Love Divine, and who is the weapon to destroy the demon of doubt.

Hail, O Lord of Men! Victory unto You!

नरदेव देव, जय जय नरदेव।
अद्वयतत्त्वसमाहितचित्तं
प्रोज्ज्वलभक्तिपटावृतवृत्तम्।
कर्मकलेवरमद्भुतचेष्टं
यामि गुरुं शरणं भववैद्यम्।।
नरदेव देव, जय जय नरदेव।।4।।

4. Hail, O Lord of Men! Victory unto you! I surrender myself to my Guru the Man-God, the physician for the malady of this Samsara (relative existence), whose mind ever dwelt on the non-dualistic Truth, whose personality was covered by the cloth of Supreme Devotion, who was ever active (for the good of humanity) and whose actions were all superhuman.

Hail, O Lord of Men! Victory unto You!

SALUTATION TO SHRI RAMAKRISHNA

स्थापकाय च धर्मस्य सर्वधर्मस्वरूपिणे।

अवतारवरिष्ठाय रामकृष्णाय ते नमः।।

I bow down to Ramakrishna, who established the religion, embodying in himself the reality of all religions and being thus the foremost of divine Incarnations.

SECTION - III

TRANSLATED FROM SWAMIJI

RUDRA-PRAYER

From the unreal lead us to the Real.
From darkness lead us unto light.
From death lead us to immortality.
Reach us through and through our self.
And evermore protect us – O Thou Terrible!
From ignorance, by Thy sweet compassionate face.

THE HYMN OF SWEETNESS

The blissful winds are sweet to us.
The seas are showering bliss on us.
May the corn in our fields bring bliss to us.
May the plants and herbs bring bliss to us.
May the cattle give us bliss.
O Father in Heaven, be Thou blissful unto us!
Thy very dust of the earth is full of bliss.
It is all bliss–all bliss–all bliss.

THE HYMN OF CREATION

Existence was not then, nor non-existence,
The world was not, the sky beyond was neither.
What covered the mist? Of whom was that?
What was in the depths of darkness thick?

Death was not then, nor immortality,
The night was neither separate from day,
But motionless did *That* vibrate

Alone, with Its own glory one –
Beyond *That* nothing did exist.

At first in darkness hidden darkness lay,
Undistinguished as one mass of water,
Then *That* which lay in void thus covered
A glory did put forth by *Tapah!*

First desire rose, the primal seed of mind,
(The sages have seen all this in their hearts
Sifting existence from non-existence.)
Its rays above, below and sideways spread.

Creative then became the glory,
With self-sustaining principle below.
And Creative Energy above.

Who knew the way? Who there declared
Whence this arose? Projection whence?
For after this projection came the gods.
Who therefore knew indeed, came out this whence?

This projection whence arose,
Whether held or whether not,
He the ruler in the supreme sky, of this
He, O Sharman! knows, or knows not
He perchance!

NIRVANASHATKAM, OR SIX STANZAS ON NIRVANA

I am neither the mind, nor the intellect, nor the ego, nor the mind-stuff;
I am neither the body, nor the changes of the body;
I am neither the senses of hearing, taste, smell, or sight,
Nor am I the ether, the earth, the fire, the air;
I am Existence Absolute, Knowledge Absolute, Bliss Absolute –
I am He, I am He. (Shivoham, Shivoham).

I am neither the Prâna, nor the five vital airs;
I am neither the materials of the body, nor the five sheaths;
Neither am I the organs of action, nor object of the senses
I am Existence Absolute, Knowledge Absolute, Bliss Absolute –
I am He, I am He. (Shivoham, Shivoham).

I have neither aversion nor attachment, neither greed nor delusion;
Neither egotism nor envy, neither Dharma nor Moksha;
I am neither desire nor objects of desire;
I am Existence Absolute, Knowledge Absolute, Bliss Absolute –
I am He, I am He. (Shivoham, Shivoham).

I am neither sin nor virtue, neither pleasure nor pain;
Nor temple nor worship, nor pilgrimage nor scriptures,
Neither the act of enjoying, the enjoyable nor the enjoyer;
I am Existence Absolute, Knowledge Absolute, Bliss Absolute –
I am He, I am He. (Shivoham, Shivoham).

I have neither death nor fear of death, nor caste;
Nor was I ever born, nor had I parents, friends, and relations;
I have neither Guru, nor disciple;
I am Existence Absolute, Knowledge Absolute, Bliss Absolute –
I am He, I am He. (Shivoham, Shivoham).

I am untouched by the senses, I am neither Mukti nor knowable;
I am without form, without limit, beyond space, beyond time;
I am in everything; I am the basis of the universe; everywhere am I.
I am Existence Absolute, Knowledge Absolute, Bliss Absolute –
I am He, I am He. (Shivoham, Shivoham).

RENUNCIATION ALONE IS FEARLESS

Alas, our minds [dally but] in imagination with palaces and pleasure gardens, and thus our lives are spent. [One's] only food is by begging–and that too is tasteless; one's bed, the dry earth; all of one's family, one's own body; and the only clothing a tattered piece of cloth around the waist–alas, still the desire for enjoyment does not leave a man.

Not knowing the power of flame,
The insect falls into it.
The fish swallows the bait,
Not knowing the hook inside.
And knowing full well the vanities
and dangers of the world,
We cannot give it up–
Such is the power of delusion.

[With rocks cooled by] the spray of the Ganga's waters,
Where the Vidyadharas love to sport–
Have such places in the Himalayas become extinct
That a man should beg (in disgrace) at others' doors?

Have the roots in the mountain forests all disappeared?
Are the springs all dry? Are the trees all withered
That bear sweet fruits and bark for garments
That a man should look with fear on the face
Of the fool whose eyebrows are dancing
[In] the wind of the pride of a little wealth?

Arise, let us go into the forest, where pure roots and fruits will be our food, pure water our only drink, and pure leaves our bed–and where the little-minded, the thoughtless, and those whose hearts are cankered with wealth do not exist.

In enjoyment is the fear of disease.
In high birth, the fear of losing caste,
In wealth, the fear of tyrants,
In honour, the fear of losing [it],
In strength, the fear of enemies.

In beauty, the fear of [old age],
In knowledge, the fear of defeat,
In virtue, the fear of scandal,
In the body, the fear of death.
In this life all is fraught with fear:
Renunciation alone is fearless.

[A person's] health [is uprooted by] thousands of [worries] and disease. Where fortune falls open a hundred gates of danger. Whosoever is born, him death will surely swallow. Say, [has] Providence ever created anything that died not?

THY LOVE I FEAR

Thy knowledge, man! I value not,
It is the love I fear;
It is thy love that shakes My throne,
Brings God to human tear.

For love, behold the Lord of all,
The formless, ever free,
Is made to take the human form
To play and live with thee.

What learning, they of Vrinda's groves,[1]
The herdsmen, ever got?
What science, girls that milked the kine?
They loved, and Me they bought.

A SONG OF SURADASA

O Lord, look not upon my evil qualities!
Thy name, O Lord, is Same-sightedness.
Make of us both the same Brahman!

One drop of water is in the sacred Yamuna,
And another is foul in the ditch by the roadside,
But, when they fall into the Ganga, both alike become holy.

So Lord, look not upon my evil qualities,
Thy name, O Lord, is Same-sightedness,
Make of us both the same Brahman!

One piece of iron is the image in the temple,
And another is the knife in the hand of the butcher,
But when they touch the philosopher's stone, both alike turn to gold.
So Lord, look not upon my evil qualities,
Thy name, O Lord, is Same-sightedness,
Make of us both the same Brahman!

NOTES

SECTION - I

IN SEARCH OF GOD: This poem forms part of a letter, written to Prof. John Henry Wright on 4th September 1893 from Salem, U.S.A. The Swami conveyed his 'heartfelt gratitude' to the professor for giving him a letter of introduction to the President of the Parliament of Religions, held at Chicago, and prefaced the poem with the remarks: 'Here are a few lines written as an attempt at poetry. Hoping your love will pardon this infliction.'

THE SONG OF THE FREE: Written to Miss Mary Hale on 15th February 1895 from New York. This poem is the first part of 'An Interesting Correspondence' *(Complete Works of Swami Vivekananda:* Vol. VIII, p. 162). The circumstances that led to this correspondence are interesting. Miss Hale had tendered him some advice not to state his position too strongly, and thus offend society. But the Swami was uncompromising. He stuck to his position and his response in his letter of first February 1895 was full of the fire of the fearless Sannyasin. This slightly hurt Miss Hale, and to assuage her feelings, the Swami wrote to her in verse, still asserting his position.

MISUNDERSTOOD: This poem also forms part of the correspondence referred to above. Not only Mary Hale, but many others misunderstood Vedanta as it was new to them. The Swami, therefore, corrected her by pointing out that Vedanta was not a pantheistic creed.

MY PLAY IS DONE: Composed on March 16, 1895 in New York.

NO ONE TO BLAME: This poem of Swamiji was presented to Swami Vijayananda, the head of the Ramakrishna Vedanta Centre, Buenos Aires, South America, by a devotee, whose desire to remain anonymous has resulted in the antecedents of the poem remaining unknown. The place and the date (New York, 16th May 1895) give us the only clue to fit in the bit of thought to that period of the Swamiji's life, when his individual worries and miseries were over, and persecutions from interested persons were yielding place to high appreciation of his message and personality; but the memories of the joy of the free life of a wandering monk were haunting him still in his leisure hours The last line is colophonic; maybe, the poem was sent to a friend as a greeting on the birth anniversary of Lord Buddha.

THE CUP: The place and date of composition are unknown. This poem refers to the Last Supper of the *New Testament*. *(Vide* St. Matthew, xxvi, 27-28.)

HOLD ON YET A WHILE, BRAVE HEART: Written to H. H. The Raja of Khetri, Rajputana. who was a devoted disciple of Swamiji.

THE SONG OF THE SANNYASIN: Composed at the retreat of Thousand Island Park, New York, in July 1895, where the Swami lived for seven weeks with some of his disciples in order to give them spiritual training. 'There were twelve of us,' a disciple writes, 'and it seemed as if Pentecostal fire descended and touched the Master. One afternoon, when he had been telling us of the glory of renunciation, of the joy and freedom of those of the ochre robe, he suddenly left us, and in a short time he had written his "Song of the Sannyasin", a very passion of sacrifice and renunciation.'

TO AN EARLY VIOLET: Written to Sister Christine from New York on 6th January 1896. Violet is the spring flower of the West. But when it blooms in late winter i.e. before the advent of Spring, it has to fight against the cold blast. The poem is meant to give encouragement to the disciple to stand up to adverse circumstances.

THE LIVING GOD: Written to an American friend from Almora (India) on 9th July 1897. This poem reflects the Swami's trend of thought during this period, which is expressed in a letter written to Miss Mary Hale on the same date: "May

I be born again and again, and suffer thousands of miseries so that I may worship the only God that exists, the only God I believe in, the sum total of all souls–and above all, my God the wicked, my God the miserable, my God the poor of all races, of all species, is the special object of my worship."

REQUIESCAT IN PACE: Composed at Almora in June 1898, in memoriam to J. J. Goodwin, who passed away at Ootacamund on 2nd June 1898. Mr. Goodwin was a young disciple of the Swami and had taken stenographic notes of most of his lectures. His passing away came as a shock to Swamiji and he felt that his days of public lecture were over. Sister Nivedita writes in her *Notes of Some Wanderings with Swami Vivekananda:* 'One day he carried off a few faulty lines of someone's writing, and brought back a poem, which was sent to the widowed mother, as his memorial of her son.'

TO THE AWAKENED INDIA: Composed at Srinagar (Kashmir) in June 1808. Written to the *Prabuddha Bha-rata* or *Awakened India,* in August 1898, when the journal was transferred from Madras to Almora, Himalayas, into the hands of the Brotherhood lounded by Swami Vivekananda. Sister Nivedita writes: 'The Swami had always had a special love for this paper, as the beautiful name he had given it indicated . ... .Day after day he would talk of the forthcoming first number, under the new editorship of Swami Swarupananda. And one afternoon he brought to us, as we sat together, a paper, on which he said, he had "tried to write a letter, but it would come this way".'

TO THE FOURTH OF JULY: On the 4th July 1898, Swami Vivekananda was travelling with some of his western disciples in Kashmir and as part of a 'domestic conspiracy' for the celebration of the day–the anni-versary of the American Declaration of Independence–he composed this poem, to be read aloud at the time of breakfast. The poem was preserved by Mrs. Ole Bull, one of the disciples of Swamiji. It is significant to note that the Swami gave up his mortal frame on the same date four years later.

KALI THE MOTHER: Composed at Kashmir in 1898. This poem was written or forced itself into writing, when, during the days of pilgrimage to Kshir Bhavani (Kashmir), the Swami was in such a high spiritual state that it seemed indeed as if his physical frame could not bear it for long.

Sister Nivedita who accompanied the Swami on that pilgrimage says: 'His brain was teeming with thoughts, he said one day, and his fingers would not rest till they were written down. It was that same evening that he came back to our house-boat from some expedition, and found waiting for us, where he had called and left them, his manuscript lines on *Kali the Mother.* Writing in a fever of inspiration, he had fallen on the floor, when he had finished–as we learnt afterwards–exhausted with his own intensity.'

ANGELS UNAWARES: Written at Calcutta in November 1898.

TO MY OWN SOUL: Written at Ridgely Manor, New York, in 1899. 'To my own Soul', the Swami said, as he handed it to Miss Josephine MacLeod.

PEACE: Composed at Ridgely Manor on 21st September 1899. Swamiji wrote this poem on the day Sister Nivedita decided to wear the nun's garb and handed it to her on her return from a drive in the evening.

WHO KNOWS HOW MOTHER PLAYS!: 'Aside from writing stories, Swamiji wrote at least one poem during his stay in Southern California. This, too, he sent to Nivedita. It was, almost certainly the beautiful and now famous poem "Who Knows How Mother Plays". Nivedita wrote on January 13, 1900: "Your birthday-poem reached me here last night." (January 12 was Swamiji's birthday.)' *(Swami Vivekananda His Second Visit to the West: New Discoveries* by Marie Louise Burke, pp. 230-31).

THOU BLESSED DREAM: Written in Paris on 17th August 1900. This poem was sent from Paris to Sister Christine (Miss Greenstidel of Detroit). The previous version of the poem differs in some respects from the present one, which is the original version and has recently come to our hands.

A BENEDICTION: Written to Sister Nivedita on 22nd September 1900 at Perros-Guiree in Brittany. Swamiji wanted that Nivedita should work out her own way without depending on him. So he blessed her through this poem in which were condensed all the hopes, aspirations, and good wishes of the Master for his disciple.

MANY HAPPY RETURNS: Written on 22nd September 1900 to Miss Alberta Sturgis for her twenty-third birthday. It was sent to her to Paris from Perros-Guirec in Brittany. The poem 'A Benediction' was also presented to Sister Nivedita on the same date. It is also significant that the first few lines of both the poems are identical. After presenting the poem to Alberta, Swamiji wrote below: 'This little poem is for your birthday. It is not good, but it has all my love. 1 am sure, therefore, you will like it.'

LIGHT: This poem forms part of a letter written to Joe (Miss Josephine MacLeod) from Belur Math on 26th December 1900.

SECTION - II

ON THE SEA'S BOSOM: Swamiji composed this poem in Bengali during his return from his second trip to the west. At the time of writing it, he was probably crossing the eastern Mediterranean.

A SONG OF CREATION: Translation of a Bengali song, composed by Swamiji. This reflects the ideas of creation contained in the *Upanishads.*

A SONG ON SAMADHI: Rendered from a Bengali song, composed by Swamiji. It gives an idea of the various stages of the mind leading up to Samadhi.

SHIVA IN ECSTASY and *THE DANCE OF SHIVA:* These are translations of the beautiful songs on Shiva, composed by Swamiji in Bengali. The first one was composed at the Baranagore Math in 1887, on the occasion of Shivaratri (the Spring worship of Shiva). The second one might have been composed during this period as it expresses the same idea.

TO SHRI KRISHNA : Rendered from Hindi. The song depicts the sweet entreaties of a cowherd-girl of Vrindaban to youth Krishna who had barred her path to the river.

TO A FRIEND: Rendered from a Bengali poem composed by Swami Vivekananda. It was first published in the *Udbodhan* (Vol. I, No. 2), Bengali monthly of the Ramakrishna Order. Swamiji's life experience has been focussed in this poem.

AND LET SHYAMA DANCE THERE: Rendered from Bengali. It was first published in the *Udbodhan* (Vol. II, No. 1). This poem can be compared with the English poem 'Kali the Mother.'

Most probably this poem was written between 13th and 19th July 1899. About this poem, Nivedita wrote to Miss Josephine MacLeod on the 13th: 'He (Swamiji) is writing a grand Bengali poem about the Mother'; and again on 19.7.1899: 'Then his great Bengali poem to Kali. Here is one line–oh, if you could see him say dramatically: –

"I am not one of those fools who
Put the garland of skulls round thy neck–
Then start with terror–and call Thee Merciful!" '

A SONG I SING TO THEE: Rendered from Bengali. It was first published in the *Udbodhan* (Vol. IV, No. 9). A certain portion of this poem is found in a letter written in summer 1894 from U.S.A. to Swami Ramakrishnananda at the Baranagore Math. The Swami wrote in the postscript: 'Keep a copy of my poem–Shall send you more later.' This poem reflects in some measure Swamiji's experiences at Ghazipur (in U.P.), where he decided to be initiated into Raja-Yoga by the saint Pavhari Baba. But he had repeated visions of Shri Ramakrishna, with an aggrieved look, for a few days and this made him drop his resolution. *(Vide* Conversations and Dialogues, *Complete Works,* Vol. VII, pp. 242-43 for more details).

A HYMN TO THE DIVINE MOTHER and *SHIVA:* Though a great Advaitin, Swamiji was a profound devotee, too. These Sanskrit hymns portray this aspect of Swamiji.

A HYMN TO THE DIVINITY OF SHRI RAMAKRISHNA : Rendered from Bengali. It is called the *āratrika* hymn. *'Aratrika'* literally means 'religious service held at night'. But it generally refers to the vesper service in Hindu temples, consisting mainly in moving lights and other adjuncts of worship before the image. At the monasteries of the Ramakrishna Order, the vesper is concluded with the *āratrika* hymn.

WHOM TO FEAR?: These stanzas in Sanskrit form part of a letter dated 25th September 1894, addressed to the Swami's brother-disciples at Baranagore. They forcefully express his fearlessness born of unflinching faith to Shri Ramakrishna.

HYMNS TO SHRI RAMAKRISHNA: These two hymns to Shri Ramakrishna were composed by Swamiji in November 1898 at the rented Math premises at Belur. Sharat Chandra Chakravarty, a lay disciple of Swamiji, has left the following record: 'Swamiji is now much engaged in the study and discussion of Sanskrit scriptures. The couplets beginning with *Achandalapratihatarayah* he composed about this time. Today Swamiji composed the hymn *Om hrim ritam* etc., and handing it over to the disciple said: "See if there is any metrical defect in these stanzas". The disciple made a copy of the poem for this purpose.

'On this day it seemed as if the Goddess of Learning has manifested herself on his tongue. With the disciple, he fluently talked for about two hours at a stretch in exceedingly melodious Sanskrit. After the disciple had copied the hymn, Swamiji said, "You see, as I write immersed in thought, grammatical slips sometimes occur; therefore I ask you all to look over them." Disciple replied: "Sir, these are not slips, but the license of genius."' *(Complete Works,* Vol. VII, pp. 132-33).

SALUTATION TO SHRI RAMAKRISHNA: Composed at the house of the late Navagopal Ghose (a householder disciple of Shri Ramakrishna), Ramakrishnapur, How-rah, on 6th February 1898. The record of the disciple runs thus: 'Today the festival of installing the image of Shri Ramakrishna was to come off at the residence of Babu Navagopal Ghose. The Sannyasins of the Math and the householder devotees of Shri Ramakrishna had all been invited there. .. .Swamiji himself conducted the worship, with Swami Prakashananda to assist him. After the worship was over, Swamiji, while still in the worship-room, composed *ex tempore* this *mantra* for prostration before Bhagavan Shri Ramakrishna.'

SECTION - III

RUDRA-PRAYER and *THE HYMN OF SWEETNESS:* The Rudra-prayer is taken from the *Yajur-Veda;* and the Hymn of Sweetness is found in the *Rig-Veda,* I. 90. 6-9, and also in the *Brihadaranyaka Upanishad,* VI. 3. 6. and the *Mahanarayana Upanishad* (Section XXXIX: Trisuparna Mantra). Swamiji translated these two hymns while on his way to Kashmir on 12th June 1898. About the translation of the Rudra-prayer, Sister Nivedita writes in her *Notes of Some Wanderings with Swami Vivekananda:* 'On Sunday afternoon, we rested, near the plains, in what we took to be an out-of-the-way hotel, above a lake and fall, and these he translated for us the Rudra-prayer. He hesitated a long time over the fourth line, thinking of rendering it. "Embrace us in the heart of our heart." But at last he put his perplexity to us saying shyly, "The real meaning is: Reach us through and through our self."'

About the Hymn of Sweetness, she writes: 'It was indeed an afternoon of translations, and he gave us fragments of the great benediction after mourning, which is one of the most beautiful of the Hindu sacraments.'

THE HYMN OF CREATION: It is a translation of Swamiji from the Nasadiya Sukta, *Rig-Veda* (X. 129). About this translation, Swamiji wrote from Mayavati to Mrs. Ole Bull on 6th January 1901: 'I send you forthwith a translation of the *Nasadiya* Hymn sent by Dr. Bose (Jagadish Chandra) through you. I have tried to make it as literal as possible.' Swamiji more than once referred to the poetic beauty of this Vedic hymn in his lectures.

NIRVANASHATKAM OR SIX STANZAS ON NIRVANA : Swamiji's translation of a poem by Shankaracharya, expressing the non-dualistic absoluteness of the Atman.

RENUNCIATION ALONE IS FEARLESS: This is a free translation of several verses (Nos. 14, 15, 18, 24-26, 31, 33) from Bhartrihari's *Vairagya Shatakam,* a Sanskrit work of medieval India. The translation is taken from a manuscript, written by Swami Vivekananda himself in October 1898 in Kashmir. Nivedita wrote in her diary: 'On Wednesday he translated for us the Hundred Verses on Renunciation.' The original was sent to the Vedanta Society of Southern California by Josephine MacLeod in 1948, just before her passing away. This title was provided by the editors of the *Vedanta and the West* (No. 163) and the words set in square brackets were supplied by Swami Madhavananda, the ninth President of the Ramakrishna Math and Mission.

THY LOVE I FEAR: Translation of a Bengali song by Swamiji. It formed part of a piece of writing by him 'The story of the Boy Gopala'. Sri Ramakrishna used to like this song very much.

A SONG OF SURADASA: According to the chronicles of Sister Nivedita, Swamiji translated this song on his way to Kashmir on 12th June 1898. This wonderful devotional song of Suradasa played an important role in his life. During his itinerary days, at Jaipur, he was invited by the Raja of Khetri to attend an entertainment of music by a nautch-girl. Being a monk, he at first refused to attend it, but when he realised the hidden meaning of this song, sung in a plaintive tune, he went to the hall of audience to hear her. He later remarked: 'That incident removed the scales from my eyes. Seeing that all are indeed the manifestation of the One, I could no longer condemn anybody.'